homes

people

park

market

road signs

pavements

roads

The town

buildings

shops

traffic

I spy something beginning with p, h, b, r, and m.

semi-detached house

old people's home

bungalow

detached house

flats

hotel

caravan

Places to live

terraced houses

shop

motel

2

The old lady likes her bungalow because it has no stairs.

This boy and girl live in a big block of flats.

This man and his family live over their shop.

This family likes to chat to the family next door.

The road

car park

attendant

pedestrian crossing

pavement

kerb

bus stop

road sweeper

drain

manhole

Keep Left

traffic island

road

traffic lights

traffic warden

road mender

The pedestrian crossing is a safe place to cross the road.

The car park is full of cars.

The children are going to school on the bus.

bus driver

bus conductor

The lorry has to stop because the traffic lights show red.

museum and
art gallery

G.P.O. (General Post Office)

school

church

Important buildings

fire station

bus station

college

police station

town hall

railway station

hospital

The boy is going in to
the hospital from the
ambulance.

The policeman is
arresting the thief.

The fire engine is rushing to
a house which is on fire.

People who run the town
meet in the town hall.

car

double-decker bus

lorry

coach

taxi

bicycle

it's quicker by bus!

Traffic

motor bike

van

scooter

fire engine

ambulance

The man is going to
the railway station
in a taxi.

This van delivers
bread to the shops.

The G.P.O. van
delivers parcels.

The lorry
delivers coal to
people's houses.

fruit and vegetable stall

jewellery stall

antique stall

fish stall

The market

meat stall

clothes stall

pots and pans

material stall

second-hand stall

toy stall

The lady is setting out her stall.

The man brings his vegetables to the market in a van.

Mother is buying fresh fish for dinner.

The boy and girl like to spend some money at the toy stall.

butcher's

carpet and furniture shop

chemist

florist and
greengrocer

Shops

newsagent

supermarket

shoe shop

ladies' and men's
outfitters

There are a lot of
people in the
butcher's shop.

Mother uses a trolley
in the supermarket.

The carpet and
furniture shop is
having a sale.

The girl is buying some
new school shoes.

tennis courts

rose garden

pets' corner

flower beds

fish pond

football field

bowling green

The park

the park keeper

children's playground

duck pond

14

Hairdressers and barbers look after our hair.

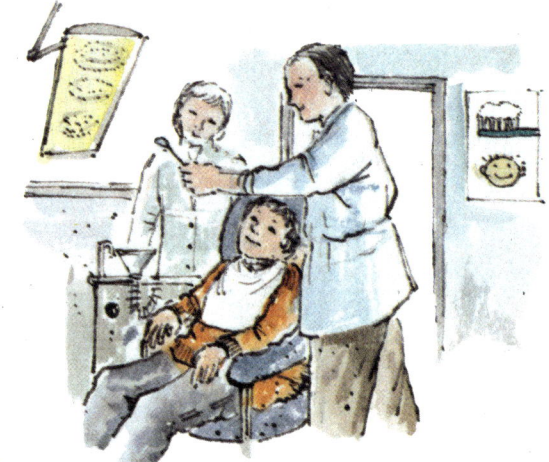

The dentist looks after our teeth.

The vet looks after our animals.

The bank looks after our money.

electrician

joiner

decorator

gas man

plumber

The builder builds houses, helped by other men.

Things to do

1 Make your own town book about your own town, village or city.
   Use this book to help you with words.
   Draw pictures of things in your own town.
   Use photographs and cut pictures from old newspapers and magazines.
   Write as much as you can in your town book.
   Draw a map to show where you live.
   Make your own book interesting and colourful.
2 Make a list of the names of any other towns you know or have visited.
3 Collect pictures of different towns.
4 Act people doing jobs round the town and guess what they are doing.